WIND ENERGY

SAVING THE PLANET THROUGH GREEN ENERGY

COLIN GRADY

Enslow Publishing
101 W. 23rd Street
Suite 240
New York, NY 10011
USA

enslow.com

Published in 2017 by Enslow Publishing, LLC.
101 W. 23rd Street, Suite 240, New York, NY 10011

Printed in China

Library of Congress Cataloging-in-Publication Data

Names: Grady, Colin, author.
Title: Wind energy / Colin Grady.
Description: New York, NY : Enslow Publishing, 2017. | Series: Saving the planet through green energy | Audience: Ages 8+. | Audience: Grades 4–6. | Includes bibliographical references and index.
Identifiers: LCCN 2016021789| ISBN 9780766082984 (library bound) | ISBN 9780766082960 (pbk.) | ISBN 9780766082977 (6-pack)
Subjects: LCSH: Wind power—Juvenile literature. | Wind turbines—Juvenile literature. | Renewable energy sources—Juvenile literature.
Classification: LCC TJ820 .G69 2017 | DDC 333.9/2—dc23
LC record available at https://lccn.loc.gov/2016021789

To Our Readers: We have done our best to make sure all website addresses in this book were active and appropriate when we went to press. However, the author and the publisher have no control over and assume no liability for the material available on those websites or on any websites they may link to. Any comments or suggestions can be sent by e-mail to customerservice@enslow.com.

Portions of this book originally appeared in the book *Wind Energy: Blown Away!* by Amy S. Hansen.

Photo Credits: Cover, ssuaphotos/Shutterstock.com (wind turbines); Mad Dog/Shutterstock.com (series logo and chapter openers); p. 6 Redchanka/Shutterstock.com; p. 7 wavebreakmedia/Shutterstock.com; p. 9 Subbotina Anna/Shutterstock.com; p. 11 John Greim/LightRocket/Getty Images; p. 14 Andrew Zarivny/Shutterstock.com; p. 16 TOBIAS SCHWARZ/AFP/Getty Images; p. 17 Spencer Platt/Getty Images News/Getty Images; p. 19 Daniel Acker/Bloomberg/Getty Images; p. 21 Thomas Imo/Photothek/Getty Images; p. 22 Cbenjasuwan/Shutterstock.com.

CONTENTS

WORDS TO KNOW

coils The rings or curls of things that are wound up.

develop To work out or form.

engineers Masters at planning and building engines, machines, roads, and bridges.

fossil fuels Fuels, such as coal, natural gas, or gasoline, that were made from plants that died millions of years ago.

generate To make.

millstones Heavy, circular stones used for making grain into a powder.

percent One part of 100.

pumps Devices that remove liquid from one place and move it to another.

ranches Large farms for raising cattle, horses, or sheep.

source The place where something starts.

turbines Motors that turn by a flow of water or air.

CHAPTER 1

WHAT IS WIND ENERGY?

We have all seen the wind in action. A flag flutters and your hair blows in the breeze. Snow turns into drifts during a blizzard. That moving air has energy. The wind's energy moves sailboats across lakes and turns wind **turbines** to make electricity. When we catch the wind's energy, we have wind power.

Moving air has energy. When we capture this energy, the wind power can be used to make electricity.

A RENEWABLE SOURCE

Most of the electricity used in the United States comes from **fossil fuels**. However, we are using the wind more and more. Wind power is a renewable energy **source**. This means that no matter how much we use, we cannot use it up. It is also a nonpolluting energy source. When we capture wind energy, we are not putting smoke or other pollution into the air.

Wind power is a clean and renewable source of power to make the electricity that we use every day.

CHAPTER 2

WHERE DOES WIND COME FROM?

When a hurricane hits, winds are faster than 75 miles (120 kilometers) per hour. The strong gusts can knock down huge trees. Softer breezes cause only a single piece of grass to flutter. Whether it is powerful or gentle, wind is here because of the sun.

As the sun's rays reach Earth, they warm up the air. However, the sun does not warm air evenly. For example, air over land heats up more quickly than air over water during the day. Pockets of air that are warmer than others cause wind. When air gets warm, it rises. Then, cooler air rushes in to take its place. This movement of air is wind. As long as the sun shines, there will be wind that we can use to power turbines, windmills, and sailboats.

The sun is the power behind wind. The sun's heat warms the air, and the air rises. Cooler air moves in, and wind blows.

WIND ENERGY IN HISTORY

Long ago, the Nile River was like a highway for ancient Egyptians. After paddling their boats downstream, Egyptians put up sails. The sails caught the wind and pushed the boats upstream. Sails are one of the earliest ways people used the wind.

Windmills are another early invention. Windmill blades catch the wind and turn. The turning blades power water **pumps** or turn **millstones**. Millstones grind wheat to make flour. Windmills were already in use in China and Persia more than one thousand years ago. Later, the Netherlands became famous for windmills that pumped seawater off land. Early American settlers used windmills, too.

This windmill was built in 1795. You can still visit it today on Cape Cod in Brewster, Massachusetts.

WIND ENERGY TIMELINE

Around 1000 BCE The Egyptians and others **develop** sailboats.

1390 CE People in the Netherlands start building windmills to pump seawater off of land.

1854 Halladay windmills are developed. They look like a wheel with paddles. The windmills are soon used for pumping water on **ranches** in the American West.

1888 In Cleveland, Ohio, Charles F. Brush builds the first windmill that generates electricity.

1977 The world is faced with an oil shortage when some countries refuse to sell their oil. Renewable energy, such as wind energy, gets more attention.

1991 The world's first offshore wind farm is built in the Baltic Sea, off the coast of Denmark.

2006 The amount of electricity generated by wind in the United States goes up 45 percent from the year before.

2008 The largest wind turbines yet built go up in Germany. One of these giant turbines can provide enough electricity for about 1,800 houses.

2016 Wind power continues to increase. The world is able to make 435,000 megawatts of power using wind. (One megawatt is equal to a million watts.)

CHAPTER 3

USING WIND TURBINES TO MAKE ELECTRICITY

A tall wind turbine can catch the wind.

We use electricity to charge our cell phones and devices, light our homes, and dry our clothes. How can the wind turn into electricity? Wind turbines are windmills that make electricity. We **generate** electricity by moving magnets around **coils** of wires. A wind turbine's job is to use the energy from the wind to move the magnets.

Wind turbines sit on top of tall towers so that they can reach the wind. A wind turbine's blades are joined to a short stick called a drive shaft. When the wind turns the blades, they turn the drive shaft. The turning drive shaft moves gears. These gears turn the generator, which spins magnets around wires. This makes electricity.

WIND FARMS

A wind farm sounds like a place to grow wind. In fact, wind farms are places that change wind into electricity. Wind farms sometimes use hundreds of wind turbines.

Wind farm turbines are big. The largest turbines have blades that are longer than a football field! A midsized turbine has blades that are 135 feet (40 meters) long. Its tower is 260

feet (79 m) tall. The Snyder Wind Project, in western Texas, has even taller turbines. Together with their towers, these turbines are taller than the Statue of Liberty. This wind farm's 421 turbines provide electricity for 220,000 houses.

Some wind farms are in the water, such as this German one in the North Sea. They can use the strong wind that blows over the water.

CHAPTER 4

RATING THE WIND

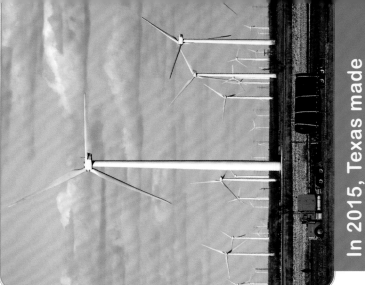

In 2015, Texas made almost 12 percent of its electricity from wind power.

Wind farms can be found all over the United States. The farms made more than 4 **percent** of the nation's electricity. Texas makes more wind power than any other state. The Block Island Wind Farm is being built in the ocean, 3 miles (5 km) off the coast of Rhode Island! What do these places have in common? They are both windy.

17

Engineers study the wind and give a wind code to each area. In the United States, the least windy places earn a one rating. The windiest places get a seven. Wind farms will work only in areas that have at least a three rating. These places tend to be in the middle of prairies or on mountains. They can also be off the coasts in the ocean.

LIGHTER WINDS

Many places do not have strong winds. However, smaller turbines can work fine there. Small turbines need less wind to work than large turbines. Some small wind turbines have blades that are only 9 feet (3 m) across. Farmers use these turbines to pump water for animals. Slightly bigger turbines make electricity for individual houses or farms.

Some wind turbines are large, like this one being lifted up to the top of its tower. But others are much smaller. Smaller turbines need less wind to work.

Other than their size, small turbines usually look just like large turbines. However, engineers are trying new designs, too. One design even looks like a coiled spring. These new designs may be able to make electricity from even lighter wind.

CHAPTER 5

THE FUTURE OF WIND ENERGY

Is wind energy a clean source of power? Can more wind power be made to power more cities? Turbines do make clean electricity, when the wind blows. However, if the wind does not blow, there is no electricity.

Electricity generated by wind power cannot be stored easily. It must be moved to where it will be used. It is hard to move electricity over long distances. Since people do not often live in the windiest areas, engineers must find ways to connect turbines and cities. The wind must also blow steadily for wind power to be successful. If the wind is really strong one day and weak the next, turbines will not work well.

Wind turbines can be far away from the people who use the power. These workers place a cable in the ground that will connect a wind farm with buildings farther away.

The moving turbines can also accidentally kill wildlife that fly into the blades. The moving blades can cause problems with television and radio signals. Finally, some people think turbines are ugly and ruin beautiful scenery.

THE PRICE OF WIND POWER

Wind power was once fairly expensive, but now the cost of it has been going down.

Generating electricity using wind power now costs just a little more than making electricity from coal. However, wind power creates none of the pollution that using coal does. Also, while fossil fuels, such as coal, are running out, wind power is renewable.

Today, many more people are buying wind turbines. Some people are buying small turbines to put on a home or farm. Big companies are buying large turbines and setting up wind farms. As wind turbines get better, we may find that some of our energy problems are blown away!

Some people are putting small wind turbines on their roofs. The turbines make electricity that they can use in their homes.

FURTHER READING

BOOKS

Centore, Michael. *Renewable Energy.* Broomall, PA: Mason Crest, 2015.

Einspruch, Andrew. *What Is Energy?* New York: PowerKids Press, 2014.

Kopp, Megan. *Energy from Wind: Wind Farming.* New York: Crabtree Publishing Co., 2016.

Otfinoski, Steven. *Wind, Solar, and Geothermal Power: From Concept to Consumer.* New York: Children's Press, 2016.

Sneideman, Joshua. *Renewable Energy: Discover the Fuel of the Future with 20 Projects.* White River Junction, VT: Nomad Press, 2016.

WEBSITES

Energy Star Kids
energystar.gov/index.cfm?c=kids.kids_index
Learn more facts about energy and how you can save energy and help the planet.

NASA's Climate Kids: Energy
climatekids.nasa.gov/menu/energy
Lots of fun facts and links about energy.

US Energy Information Administration
eia.gov/kids
Read about the history of energy, get facts about types of energy, learn tips to save energy, and link to games and activities.

INDEX